Decision Making

PEG SERIES
(Practical Exercises for Groups)
General Series Editor: Humphrey Shaw

The PEG Series is designed to improve managers' (and trainee managers') analytical and problem solving, decision making and presentational skills. Most titles in the Series include compuer disk simulations for group use, case studies and supporting Trainer's Manuals which contain model answers, notes, transparencies, and other training support material.

Decision Making, the first in the Series, comprises:
This book of case studies

plus, accompanying

Trainer's Manual

Suggested model answers to the case studies, overhead projection transparencies and other supporting material. isbn 0 946139 47 4 £49.99

also

House Building Management Simulation
Trainer's Manual and computer simulation for group training on the management of property development. isbn 0 946139 19 9 £99.99
(educational edition isbn 0 946139 29 6 £49.99)

Football Management Simulation
Trainer's Manual and computer simulation for group training based on football team management. isbn 0 946139 09 1 £99.99
(educational edition isbn 0 946139 24 5 £49.99)

Restaurant Management Simulation
trainer's Manual and computer simulation for group training on the running of a restaurant. isbn 0 946139 14 8 £99.99
(educational edition isbn 0 946139 34 2 £49.99)

All software is priced without VAT which must be added.

Decision making

Case Studies in Financial and Quantitative Management

Humphrey Shaw

Brian Dakin   **Jon Carter**   **Wayne Griffiths**

SERIES

c Humphrey Shaw, March 1989

This first edition of Decision Making has been published by ELM Publications of 12 Blackstone Road, Huntingdon PE18 6EF (Tel. 0480-414553/Fax 0480-433577) on May 31st, 1989.

British Library Cataloguing in Publication Data
Decision-making.
   1. Financial management. Decision making
  I. Shaw, Humphrey II. Series
  658.1'51

  ISBN 0 - 946139 - 42 - 3

Printed in Great Britain by
St Edmundsbury Press Limited, Bury St Edmunds, Suffolk

CONTENTS

About the authors vi
Dedication vii
Table of case study topics viii
Introduction xi
Cautionary note xiii

CASE STUDIES

R and J Builders 1
Gardener's Friend 2
Rohan Industries 3
Good Food Supermarkets 5
Leather Goods Limited 6
Manakos Limited 8
Ankar Limited 9
Electric Motors Limited 10
Lang Couriers Limited 11
Jones Haulage Limited 12
Auto Factors 13
Johnstone Building Supplies 14
The Angler Free House 15
The Shoe Factory 16
Sioux Adventure Limited 17
Hair Style 18
Zepal Limited 20
RKT Limited 22
Leisure Time 25
John and Sarah Harrison 29
Sounds Right 37
ZZX Limited and AOT Limited 39
The Handy Chemist 40
Highways Construction 42
Beese Engineering Limited 44
Air Freight Packers Limited 46
Hyde Engineering Limited 53
The Thistle Wool Company Limited 56
Sarah Jane Limited 66
Blenheim Road Garages Limited 70

Summary of the accounting ratios in common use 79
Prescribed formats for company accounts 82
Profit and loss account - formats 1 and 2 84
Glossary 86
DCF Tables 91

ABOUT THE AUTHORS

Humphrey Shaw is Senior Lecturer in Accounting and Finance at the Business School, Polytechnic of North London.

Brian Dakin, Jon Carter and Wayne Griffiths have acted as Consultant Programmers for the software simulations on computer disk which accompany this Book and its Trainer's Manual.

To

Phoebe Shaw

Table of Case Study Topics

Case	Topic
R & J Builders	Accounting Concepts
Gardener's Friend	Ledger Accounts Trial Balance Profit & Loss A/C
Rohan	Trial Balance
Good Food Supermarkets	Z Charts
Leather Goods	Manufacturing Accounts
Manakos	Cost Behaviour
Ankar	Labour Costing
Electric Motors Ltd	Flexible Budgets
Lang Couriers	Statistical Regression
Jones Hauliers	Statistical Regression Depreciation
Auto Factors	Stock Control
Johnstone Building Supplies	Cash Budgets
Angler Freehouse	Break Even
Shoe Factory	Break Even
Sioux Adventure	Trend Analysis
Hair Style	Correlation Discounted Cash Flow

ix

Case	Topic
Zepal	Source & Application
RKT	Source and Application Presentation of Data using computer software
Leisure Time	Ratio Analysis
John & Sarah Harrison	Ratio Analysis Business Appraisal
Sounds Right	Linear Programming
ZZX and AOT	Capital Structure
Handy Chemist	Random Numbers
Highway Construction	Node Network
Beese Engineering	Node Network
Air Freight Packers	Source and Application Consolidated Accounts Bank Lending
Hyde Engineering	Financial Negotiating
Thistle Wool	Company Acquisitions Negotiating
Sarah Jane	Measures of Central Tendency Break Even Correlation Raising of Finance Financial Ratios
Blenheim Road Garages	Linear Programming Budgetary Control Source & Application Probability Break Even

X

Introduction

Financial Management and Quantitative Management Techniques have become two very important subjects on business and management courses. Managers spend a large part of their working life making decisions often under conditions of uncertainty. An understanding of financial management and quantitative techniques allows managers to select the best decision from a number of variables.

This book of case studies has been written with the aim of helping you to learn more about these two subjects while at the same time helping you to improve your decision making. The book is divided into two sections. The first part allows you to use your knowledge to solve problems which are based around one topic. It is intended that students will work on these cases on their own to improve their techniques. The next section presents the student in the role of manager dealing with a variety of problems in which an understanding of financial and quantitative techniques can help in the decision making progress. These cases have been written for group work because managers spend most of their time making decisions in meetings. These cases therefore allow the business and management student to practice their inter-personal skills.

Many of the cases require the student to present their findings both orally and in report format.

I would like to thank all the staff at the Thames Valley College of Higher Education who have helped me with these case studies particularly John Congram FCCA and Ron Webb FCCA. Lastly I would like to thank Douglas Smith BA of Watford College, Helena Shaw BA PhD Dacorum College, Geoff Bath MSc Hatfield Polytechnic, Sally Messenger BSc MSc Surrey University and Derek Belcher Managing Director Universal Packing for their many useful suggestions.

If you owe £50, you're a delinquent account.

If you owe £50,000, you're a small business.

If you owe £50 million, you're a corporation.

If you owe £50 billion, you're the government.

L.T. White

R and J Builders

R and J Builders is a small firm of builders situated in Ludlow. The two brothers Robert and John Lepley, who manage the business, have submitted their ledgers to their accountant and written a letter asking for the following matters to be reflected in their final accounts;

a   in May we spent £5,000 on an advertising campaign and would like to spread this cost over the next three financial years

b   our headquarters were revalued in January of this year by a chartered surveyor. In 1979, when we started the business, we paid £25,000 for our premises but they have now been revalued at £37,000. Can this gain be included in this year's profit and loss account?

c   in June of last year we became a subcontractor on a new housing development on the outskirts of Ludlow. Unfortunately, there have been problems with planning permission which has delayed work and, as a result, we anticipate loosing £7,000 when the contract is completed during the next financial year. Is it possible to charge the anticipated loss to this year's accounts?

Memo   **To Accounts Assistant**

From   **Senior Partner**

I am preparing the accounts for the Lepley brothers and would be pleased if you could draft a letter to them explaining how their proposals must be treated so that their accounts comply with current accounting concepts and conventions.

1

Gardener's Friend

Gardener's Friend is a subsidiary company of Sheffield Metal Industries PLC formed five years ago, to manufacture high quality stainless steel garden tools. The firm has built up a good reputation for its tools both with the trade and the general public.

You have just joined Gardener's Friend as a trainee accountant and have been asked to prepare the ledger accounts, trial balance and costing profit and loss account for the Finance Director when he meets the main Board in two weeks time to report on the firm's financial position. The cost ledger shows the following balances.

	£
General Ledger Control Account	86,000
Materials Control Account	21,000
Work in Progress Control Account	35,000
Finished Goods Control Accounts	30,000

During the first half of the financial year the following transactions took place:

Raw materials purchased on credit	26,000
Sales on Credit	90,000
General Operating Expenses	9,000
Wages Net 9,600	
Total Wages Gross	12,000

Depreciation at 10% on fixed assets was £30,000 and the balance of the raw materials control was £14,000 after charging £2,000 to production overheads.

A notional charge for rent was made for £1,000 and indirect wages amounted to £3,000. The cost of goods sold amounted to £80,000 and the firm had accrued expenses of £1,000. It is the firm's policy to absorb overheads at 200% of direct wages. Lastly, transfers to finished goods amounted to £70,000.

Rohan Industries

Rohan Industries manufacture steel tubing which is used in the construction industry. You have just joined the company as a trainee accountant and have been given the following balances for the last financial year and asked to produce the firm's trial balance.

Balances at the start of the year:

	£000	£000
Raw materials in stock	56	
Work in progress	21	
Finished goods stock	48	
Debtors	66	
Trade Creditors		51
Expense Creditors		17
Bank	64	
Freehold Buildings	260	
Plant and Machinery	185	
Provision for depreciation		
Plant and Machinery		68
Issued Share Capital		500
Reserves		64
	700	700

Summary of Transactions During the Year

£000

Materials purchased	216
Materials issued to production	192
Materials issued to maintenance	19
Materials returned to suppliers	2
Carriage inwards	25
Factory wages	106
Factory salaries and indirect wages	48
Salaries administration	62
Salaries sales department	42
Salaries and wages distribution	19
PAYE deductions from salaries and wages	20
Payments to Collector of Taxes	16

Expenses:		
	Factory	39
	Administration	25
	Sales	43
	Distribution	12

Cheques paid to trade creditors	212
Cheques drawn from salaries and wages	248
Cheques drawn for expense creditors	155
Cheques received from debtors	868
Factory overhead absorbed	150
Provision for depreciation	30
Output completed	445
Finished goods sold	443
Sales on credit	900

Good Food Supermarkets

The Sales Director of Good Food Supermarkets is currently preparing for the Annual Managers Sales Conference. He has received the sales figures from the accounts department and last year's figures reflect the investment which the firm made in five new superstores at the end of the financial year 1985/86.

You work in the firm's Head Office and have been asked by the Sales Director to prepare a Z chart from the following figures which can be used at the Annual Sales Conference.

	1986/87	1987/88
	£m Sales	£m Sales
January	35	70
February	28	85
March	34	93
April	42	97
May	46	91
June	50	96
July	48	85
August	44	78
September	52	84
October	57	92
November	61	102
December	72	111

Leather Goods Limited

The Directors of Leather Goods have just completed their first year of trading. The company was set up to produce a range of leather goods but spent the first year manufacturing men's leather wallets because the firm received an order for 55,170 wallets from a wholesaler.

The company has just received its Manufacturing, Trading and Profit and Loss Accounts from its accountants and have asked you, as a freelance financial accountant, to explain and analyse their accounts.

Leather Goods Limited
Manufacturing, Trading and Profit and Loss
Account for Year ending 31 March 1988.

	£	£
Sales		372,397
Opening Stock of raw materials	27,250	
Purchase of raw materials	115,732	
	142,982	
Less closing stock of raw materials	34,321	
Raw materials used in production	108,661	
Direct labour	78,300	
Prime cost	186,961	
Production Overheads		
Factory Power	22,210	
Indirect labour	34,000	
Factory consumables	2,700	
Factory Rates	17,300	
Depreciation Plant		
& Machinery	4,700	80,910
		267,871
Add opening stock of W.I.P		27,500
		295,371
Less closing stock of W.I.P		42,234
Factory Cost of Goods Produced		253,137
Opening Stock of finished goods		34,720
Factory Cost of Goods Produced		253,137
		287,857
Less Closing Stock of finished goods		39,732
Cost of goods sold		248,125
Gross Profit		124,272
Gross Profit		124,272
Administration Expenses	29,732	
Selling Expenses	37,249	
Interest payments	4,300	
Total expenses		71,281
Net Profit		52,991

Manakos Limited

Manakos is a small engineering firm. The company makes a range of steel tubing. Product line Z196A sells for £9.00 per one metre unit. Unfortunately the firm's accountant has been taken ill but you have been able to find out the first quarter's production and costs of Z196A.

First Quarter Production and Costs for Product Z196A

Month	January	February	March
	£	£	£
Prime Cost	83,000	99,600	106,240
Production Overhead	44,750	50,600	52,940
Output in Units	25,000	30,000	32,000

The Marketing Manager has received an additional order for 12,000 bars from a French firm provided that the selling price can be reduced by 15%. He would like you to send him a memo showing a break down of the costs of production and a statement saying whether or not the order should be accepted.

Ankar Limited

Ankar Limited are about to enter into a local productivity agreement. The management and union negotiators have asked for an adjournment and you have been asked to calculate whether or not the firm should agree to the union's proposal or stick to its offer of a straightforward 10% pay rise. The union's proposal is as follows:

Every direct worker would receive a bonus of £0.16 for every good unit produced thereby enabling the firm to increase production by 121/2 per cent. The Marketing Director has confirmed that the increased output can be sold if the selling price of all sales is reduced by £0.20 per unit.

You have just been given next year's budget which has not taken account of any salary or wage rise.

		£000
Sales (4,000,000) units		1,600
Direct Materials	320	
Direct Wages	480	
Variable Production Overhead	72	
Fixed Production Overhead	134	
Variable Selling Overhead (5% of sales value)	80	
Fixed Selling Overhead	53	
Variable Distribution Overhead	64	
Fixed Distribution and Administration Overhead	183	
		1,386
Profit		214

9

Electric Motors Limited

Electric Motors Limited manufactures electric motors which it sells both at home and abroad. Last month the firm heard that it had lost an export tender and, as a result, has had to sell some surplus plant and reduce productive capacity to 7650 units, which represents 90% of the maximum.

You work in the Costing Department at Electric Motors and have already prepared a flexible budget covering 80%, 90% and 100% activity levels for the firm.

Flexible Budget

	80%	90%	100%
	£	£	£
Direct Materials	115,600	130,050	144,500
Direct Labour	74,800	84,150	93,500
Overheads	143,800	146,775	149,750
Sales	353,600	397,800	442,000

You have just received a memo from the Marketing Director informing you that the projected sales figure for the coming year has been reduced, since losing the export order, to 70% level of activity. As a result, she has asked you to prepare a statement in marginal costing form, showing the forecast profit for the coming year.

10

Lang Couriers Limited

Lang Couriers' Board of Directors have just decided to purchase seven motor bikes for delivering important documents in London. The firm has just negotiated a £17,500 interest only bank loan which is repayable in four years time. The Finance Director has decided to repay the borrowed capital by setting up a sinking fund and setting aside a sum of money each year. She believes that the firm can earn a 9% return and has asked you, as the firm's accountant, to calculate what sum Lang must set aside each year to repay the loan.

Jones Haulage Limited

Jones Haulage have just purchased a new lorry for £36,000. The Transport Manager has estimated that it will have a life of six years and that, at the end of that time, it will have no residual value. He has asked you, the firm's accountant, to set up a sinking fund so that in six years time the company will be able to purchase a replacement vehicle which he estimates will cost £57,000.

In the past the firm has been able to earn a 7% return on money invested and you have decided to base your calculations on that figure. How much money must the firm set aside each year to cover depreciation and the expected replacement cost of the new vehicle?

Auto Factors

Auto Factors is a small motor accessory shop which sells to the general public and the trade. Its two best-selling lines are spark plugs and oil filters. The firm is currently setting its stock levels for the coming year. The manager has asked you to calculate:

a   Auto Factors maximum, minimum and re-order and average stock levels for both products.

b   the shop's stock turnover rate for both products

c   to write him a memo outlining how the firm's stock turnover rate influences profit margins.

Budgeted Sales

Month	Spark Plugs	Oil Filters
January	1000	400
February	1400	450
March	1300	600
April	1600	670
May	1700	900
June	2200	800
July	1800	1020
August	1900	1000
September	1450	700
October	1550	650
November	1670	800
December	1200	750

Delivery Period	Spark Plugs (weeks)	Oil Filters (weeks)
Maximum	3	4
Average	2	3
Minimum	1	2
Re-Order Quantity	500	250

13

Johnstone Building Supplies

You work as the accountant for Johnstone Building Supplies. Last week you received a letter from the bank manager asking if the firm wants to renew its £6,000 overdraft facility. As a result, you have decided to prepare the firm's monthly cash budget for the third quarter and have received details of budgeted sales and purchases.

Budgeted sales are:

July	£50,400
August	£52,920
September	£57,960
October	£60,480
November	£65,520
December	£55,440

Past experience has taught you that 10% of all sales are for cash and that two thirds of credit sales are paid for in the month after sale and the remainder during the following month. Credit sales were £30,996 and £32,886 in May and June respectively.

The Purchasing Manager has told you that purchases are paid for in the month following purchase and that June's purchases amounted to £45,360. It has been decided to reduce the stock in trade at the end of each month to a level sufficient to cover the following two months' sales. In June stock in trade amounted to £90,720.

JBS prices goods to give a 331/3% gross profit on cost.

Other payments in the period are:

	July £	August £	September £
Salaries and wages	6,048	6,426	6,930
Rates	1,008	-	-
Rent	1,890	1,890	1,890
Other Expenses	2,016	2,268	2,520

In July the company had a credit balance of £20,000 on its current account.

14

The Angler Free House

The Angler Free House is a country public house situated in a small village in Gloucestershire near the River Severn. The pub used to belong to a major brewery but they sold it in 1983 to Mr and Mrs Anderson as part of the brewery's rationalisation programme. The Anderson's have built up the trade at the pub by providing excellent lunches and by creating an attractive beer garden overlooking the river.

The pub had been built with two cellars and the Andersons are proposing to set up a restaurant in one of them. A quote for £15,000 has been received from a local builder to rennovate the cellar and the Andersons estimate that a further £3,000 would have to be spent on furniture and fittings. This cost would be capitalised and written off over six years. Once completed, the restaurant could seat thirty people and the owners intend to provide a range of three course meals which would be priced at £9.99 per person. The running costs have been estimated as follows:

Estimated Costs of the Restaurant

Cost of food per person	**£3.50**
Labour (per evening)	**£50.00**
Variable Overheads (per evening)	**£16.00**

It is intended to open the restaurant every day except for Christmas Day and Boxing Day.

The Andersons have engaged your services as a freelance consultant to calculate whether the restaurant would make a viable investment proposition. They have asked you to:

a   calculate the number of meals which must be served per week to break even

b   calculate whether or not the restaurant could accept groups of twelve or more people at the reduced price of £8.00

c   to calculate the restaurant's profit assuming that it serves 160 meals per week for 52 weeks.

The Shoe Factory

The Shoe Factory was established in 1979 by Amanda Marshall. She believed that there was a demand for English fashion shoes and rented a small unit in Northampton. At first, the firm had to rely on Italian designers but since 1983 about 40% of the shoes are of British design. The shoes are sold under the brand name of Lady Amanda and are attractively priced.

As part of the Autumn collection, the firm is launching four new styles. The costs and expected sales are shown below:

Model Number	456TN	843AS	259Q	61OUZ
Selling Price (£)	23	15	32	27
Leather	6	4	10	9
Labour	8	5	9	11
Design	1	1	2	1
Expected Sales	2,000	3,500	1,400	5,900
Fixed Costs per batch of shoes (£)	2,900	4,600	6,500	1,800

Memo

To   *Accountant*

From   *Amanda*

I am enclosing information on our new Autumn range of shoes. I would be pleased if you could work out the break-even point in units for each style so that I can use this information to determine the promotional budget.

Sioux Adventure Limited

Sioux Adventure Ltd is a firm which specialises in arranging adventure holidays in North America and Canada. Every year, they arrange holidays for people who wish to go canoeing, rock climbing, horse riding and sailing in America and Canada.

The majority of holiday bookings are made during January and February but every year the firm has to forecast the number of people who will want to travel to America and Canada for adventure holidays. As a result, Sioux books accommodation in March for June, July, August and September. The firm pays 10% at the time of booking and the balance in the month for which the accommodation is booked. The payments which the firm will have to make this year are given below:

Month	US Dollars	Canadian Dollars
June	1,750,550	900,000
July	1,960,230	827,152
August	2,420,003	1,745,327
September	605,702	725,291

You work in the Management Information Department of Sioux Adventure Ltd. One of your tasks in January is to record the exchange rate of sterling against the US and Canadian dollar and calculate the trend for the coming months. The firm has always done this by recording the spot rate for buying American and Canadian dollars during the months of January and February, and then recommending to the Managing Director whether or not the firm should cover its position by buying forward or dealing in the spot market when the payments are to be made.

Hair Style

Hair Style is a successful chain of hairdressing and beauty therapy shops based in and around the Midlands. The firm has been in existence for seven years and opened its first shop in Wolverhampton. Hair Style currently has eight shops. Their size and the number of people employed in each for the current financial year are shown in the table below:

Place	Shop Size	Takings	Employees
Northampton	500 sq ft	£85,000	3
Solihull	900 sq ft	£110,000	5
West Bromwich	750 sq ft	£75,000	7
Birmingham	1500 sq ft	£140,000	9
Sheffield	800 sq ft	£90,000	6
Nottingham	3000 sq ft	£283,000	12
Wolverhampton	300 sq ft	£50,000	3
Milton Keynes	4500 sq ft	£420,000	17

The firm is currently considering three sites in the town centre of Worcester, all in the shopping precinct. The Directors believe that they are all well situated and offer the same potential, have costed each site, and estimated each shop's takings for the next three years. These are shown in the table over:

Shop Size	Cost	Working Capital	Takings
600 sq ft	£27,000	£5,000	Year 1 £17,000 Year 2 £32,000 Year 3 £52,000
1700 sq ft	£42,000	£7,000	Year 1 £24,000 Year 2 £37,000 Year 3 £52,000
5000 sq ft	£87,000	£12,000	Year 1 £35,000 Year 2 £58,000 Year 3 £74,000

At the last board meeting the Directors decided to ask a local firm of management consultants called Management Solutions to look at their figures and assess which site would make the best investment proposition. The Hair Style Directors never invest unless they can earn a return of 5% over the 3 month inter bank rate which prevails at the time of the investment decision.

Task

You work for Management Solutions and have been asked to assess the best site and to give your reasons.

Zepal Limited

You are employed as the Corporate Treasurer of Zepal Limited. The company manufactures steel castings which are used by the construction industry.

Zepal's Board of Directors are currently considering expanding their operations by purchasing a French company, situated in the Isle de France region, close to Paris. The region has been declared a Development Area by the French Government and Zepal's Board of Directors feel that the development of the area will lead to an increase in the demand for their products.

The Managing Director has just received the firm's unaudited accounts for the first six months of trading. He has sent you a memo, together with the firm's Source and Application of Funds statement, and has asked you to write a report to all Board members about the company's present financial position.

Zepal Limited

Statement of Source and Application of Funds
for the first six months of trading:
Jan-June 1989

Source of Funds

	£000	£000
Profit before taxation		705
Adjustment for Items not involving the movement of funds:		
Depreciation		<u>132</u>
Funds generated from operations		837

Application of Funds

Dividends	20	
Taxation paid	65	
Purchase of Freehold office	750	
Purchase of Plant	<u>120</u>	(955)
		<u>(118)</u>

Movements in Working Capital

Increase in Stock		170	
Increase in Debtors		245	
Decrease in Cash Balance	(63)		
Increase in Overdraft	(234)	(297)	<u>(118)</u>

RKT Limited

RKT Limited is a small firm, situated outside Truro, which specialises in the design and manufacture of high quality speakers. You work for the firm's accountants and have just received the following memo from one of the senior partners.

To   *Accounts Department*

From   *Senior Partner*

Please find, enclosed, the audited accounts for RKT Limited. The firm would like us to use one of our computer graphic packages to show their financial performance.

I will leave it up to your discretion, but I think some pie charts and bar charts would be useful. Also can you please get one of your staff to draw up a Source and Application of Funds statement so that this can also be included with their final accounts.

The following draft sheets are available for RKT Ltd the two years as at 31 March 1988 and 31 March 1987.

RKT Balance Sheet as at 31 March 1988

	1988 £	1988 £	1987 £	1987 £
FIXED ASSETS				
Land - at cost				
Buildings -				
at valuation less		15,000		10,000
depreciation		50,000		50,000
Plant - at cost less				
depreciation		20,000		15,000
Investments - at valuation		50,000		40,000
		135,000		115,000
CURRENT ASSETS				
Stocks	47,000		10,000	
Debtors & prepayments	4,500		7,600	
Short-term bills			750	
Banks and cash	15,000		13,250	
		66,500		31,600
CURRENT LIABILITIES				
Trade creditors & accruals	12,000		4,500	
Dividends proposed	5,700		4,300	
Corporation tax	15,400		12,000	
Capital gains tax	13,500			
ACT on proposed dividends	2,445		1,845	
		49,045		22,645
NET CURRENT ASSETS		17,455		8,955
PROVISIONS				
Deferred taxation	(2,000)		(3,000)	
Less: ACT recoverable	2,445		1,845	
		445		(1,155)
LONG TERM CREDITORS				
10% Debentures - 1997		(40,000)		(10,000)
9% Debentures - 1987				(30,000)
		112,900		82,800
SHAREHOLDERS' FUNDS				
£1 Ordinary shares		50,000		50,000
Revaluation reserve		32,000		2,000
Revenue reserve		30,900		30,800
		112,900		82,800

The draft profit and loss account for the ending 31st March 1988 appears as follows:

	£
Loss before taxation	(11,300)
Taxation	(14,400)
	(25,700)
Extraordinary income	45,000
less: taxation	(13,500)
	31,500
	5,800
Dividends - proposed	5,700
Retained profit	100

The following information is also available:

1. Land at a cost of £10,000 was bought during the year. Existing land held by the company was sold during the year and the profit on sales arising treated as an extraordinary item.

2. Buildings: no acquisitions or disposals arose during the year.

3. Plant costing £20,000 was acquired during the year - and due to overdepreciation in prior years all plant is revalued by £10,000.

4. Investments worth £10,000 were sold at their 1987 revalued book amounts, and thus no profit or loss arose on the disposals. No new investments were acquired.

Leisure Time

Leisure Time is a company which specialises in the retailing of sports equipment. It currently has two shops, one based in Chester and the other in Manchester.

The firm has just finalised its end of year accounts, and is considering investing in a new store in Harrogate. The Directors have found a freehold site and would like to purchase it but realise that the firm would have to raise additional capital. The new shop would cost £112,000 and require an additional £7,000 to refurbish it plus £40,000 in new stock.

The Directors believe that their company would make an attractive investment proposition for higher rate tax payers wishing to invest under the Business Expansion Scheme. They have decided to approach Finance for Expansion, a firm specialising in providing venture capital, next week to discuss their proposition and have sent you a copy of their last year's accounts.

Leisure Time
Balance Sheet as at 31 March, 1988

	£000	£000	£000
Fixed Assets:			
Land & Buildings at cost		80	
depn		10	70
Motor vehicles at cost		75	
depn		35	40
Equipment at cost		90	
depn		40	50
			160
Investments at cost			60
Current Assets:			
Stock		40	
Debtors		75	
Cash		5	
		120	
Current Liabilities:			
Creditor	50		
Taxation	35		
Proposed Dividends	25		
		110	10
			230
10% Debentures 1997			70
			160
Issued Share Capital:			
75,000 Ordinary £1 shares			75
20,000 5% Preference Shares £1 each			20
			95
Capital Reserves			24
Profit and Loss Account			41
			160

Note:
The authorised share capital is 100,000 ordinary £1 shares and 50,000 5% Preference Shares of £1 each.

LEISURE TIME

Profit and Loss Account for the year
ended 31st March 1988

	£000	£000
Sales		250
Cost of Sales		155
Gross Profit		95
Selling expenses	33	
Administrative expenses	10	
Debenture Interest	7	
		50
		45
Investment Income		15
NET PROFIT BEFORE TAXATION		60
Taxation		24
		36
Proposed Dividends:		
Ordinary	24	
Preference	1	
		25
PROFIT RETAINED		11
Retained profit brought forward		30
Retained profit at end of year		41

NOTE:

Cost of Sales includes depreciation of £15,000 on equipment.
Selling Expenses include depreciation of £10,000 on motor vehicles.
Administration expenses include depreciation of £5,000 on land and buildings.

To: *The Manager, B.E.S.*

From: *Director*

We have received an enquiry from the Directors of Leisure Time about the possibility of raising additional capital under the B.E.S. I am meeting them next week and would like you to prepare reports on the following:

1. *Identify the ratios which are relevant to a shareholder, a debenture holder and a creditor, so that I can determine whether or not their proposal to seek finance under the B.E.S. would be attractive to new investors.*

2. *Write a report outlining the terms of the B.E.S. and whether or not leisure time qualify as a company able to raise money in this way.*

3. *Write a report suggesting other ways of raising money for expansion.*

John and Sarah Harrison

John Elliot used to work as an electrical engineer for a small firm of Dynamo Manufacturers in Wolverhampton. He had been with the company for twelve years but when they lost a government contract, John was one of the staff made redundant. He feels that, because he is 53, he will not find employed work again.

He and his wife Sarah, have one daughter, Emma, who is 16 and wants to go to University once she has completed her A levels.

John and Sarah would like to take advantage of the Government Business Start-up Scheme and are currently considering three possible business ventures. The first is to set up a landscape gardening business, and the second a contract cleaning company. Both of these businesses would be located in Wolverhampton and run from the family home. The Harrisons are also prepared to sell their home, and buy a small farm in Cornwall, and convert the barns into holiday flats which they would rent out during the holiday season.

Last month, the family went to see Mr Kewley, a partner in a local firm of Accountants who specialise in helping people to start new business ventures.

At the meeting Mr Kewley took details of estimated sales and expenses and has drawn up the budgeted first accounts and estimated bank balances for each venture. You work as Mr Kewley's assistant and have just received the following memo.

To   Accounts Assistant

From   Mr Kewley

Please find enclosed the accounts for three possible business ventures. Write me a report which:

a   analyses the three ventures from a financial standpoint and choose the one which is the most attractive

29

b   *explain what the business enterprise initiative is and whether or not the Harrisons would be eligible for help under it*

c   *explain what working capital is and what steps the Harrisons should take to conserve it during the first year of trading.*

Budgeted Trading Profit & Loss Account for the year ending 31st December 1989
for Business Opportunity One - Gardening Concern

		£	£
Sales			82,846.25
Purchases		41,477.00	
Less stock at 31.12.89		2,241.08	
Cost of Sales			39,235.92
Gross Profit (or Loss)			43,610.33

LESS OPERATING EXPENDITURE:

		£	£
Telephone		300.00	
Advertising		778.26	
Stationery & Postage		274.69	
Insurance:	Business	903.49	
	Vehicles	235.00	
Fuel:	Equipment	304.35	
	Vehicles	621.85	
Servicing:	Equipment	275.00	
	Vehicles	125.00	
Depreciation:	Equipment	379.39	
	Vehicles	1,006.25	
	Office Equipment	53.75	
Vehicle Expenses		100.00	
Professional Consultants		125.00	
Bank Interest		175.00	
Partners' Drawings		30,000.00	
Total Operating Expenditure			35,657.03
Profit (or Loss) on Ordinary Activities			7,953.30

Budgeted Bank Balances from 1st Jan to 31st Dec 1989
for Business Opportunity One - Gardening Concern

	JAN	FEB	MAR	APR
Bank Balance	(484.93)	(856.72)	(1,228.51)	(1,708.69)

	MAY	JUN	JUL	AUG
Bank Balance	(2,080.48)	(373.53)	3,903.76	8,289.43

	SEP	OCT	NOV	DEC
Bank Balance	12,675.11	14,573.67	1,4201.88	13,830.09

Start up Capital required:

Owner's capital	£10,000
Overdraft	£3,000

Budgeted Trading Profit & Loss Account for the year ending 31st December 1989
for Business Opportunity Two - Cleaning Concern

		£	£
Sales			47,000.00
Purchases		8,350.00	
Less stock at 31.12.89		76.00	
Cost of Sales			8,274.00
Gross Profit (or Loss)			38,726.00

LESS OPERATING EXPENDITURE:

Telephone		500.00	
Advertising		578.26	
Stationery & Postage		274.69	
Insurance:	Business	903.49	
	Vehicles	235.00	
Fuel:	Vehicles	721.85	
Servicing:	Equipment	0.00	
	Vehicles	125.00	
Depreciation:	Equipment	417.54	
	Vehicles	656.25	
	Office Equipment	53.75	
Vehicle Expenses		100.00	
Professional Consultants		125.00	
Miscellaneous Expenditure (Accruals)		175.00	
Partners Drawings		30,000.00	
Total Operating Expenditure			34,865.83
Profit (or Loss) on Ordinary Activities			3,860.17

Budgeted Bank Balances from 1st Jan to 31st Dec 1989
for Business Opportunity Two - Cleaning Concern

	JAN	FEB	MAR	APR
Bank Balance	(726.53)	(166.58)	924.25	1,906.69

	MAY	JUN	JUL	AUG
Bank Balance	2,997.52	3,944.59	4,927.02	6,017.84

	SEP	OCT	NOV	DEC
Bank Balance	7,108.66	8,091.09	9,181.918	10,272.73

Start up Capital required:

Owner's capital	£8,000
Overdraft	£1,500

Budgeted Trading Profit & Loss Account for the year ending 31st December 1989
for Business Opportunity Three - Site/Holiday Farm Cottages

		£	£
Sales			280,037.00
Purchases		176,406.77	
Less stock at 31.12.89		2,326.55	
Cost of Sales			174,080.22
Gross Profit (or Loss)			105,956.78

LESS OPERATING EXPENDITURE:

		£	£
Telephone		400.00	
Advertising		500.00	
Stationery & Postage		274.69	
Insurance:		3,250.00	
Depreciation:	Equipment	553.75	
	Tractor	2,125.00	
	Fixtures & Fittings	1,900.00	
	Land & Buildings	3,200.00	
Veterinary Fees		1,000.00	
Rent & Rates		3,000.00	
Legal & Professional Consultants		3,325.00	
Maintenance Costs: Buildings		1,400.00	
Wages & Salaries		9,500.00	
Miscellaneous Expenditure		875.00	
Partners Drawings		16,800.00	
Total Operating Expenditure			48,103.44
			57,853.34
Interest:	Loan	4,680.00	
	Other Bank Charges	3,750.00	
			8,430.00
Profit (or Loss) on Ordinary Activities			49,423.34

Budgeted Bank Balances from 1st Jan to 31st Dec 1989
for Business Opportunity Three - Site/Holiday Farm Cottages

	JAN	FEB	MAR	APR
Bank Balance	1,903.38	(967.58)	(3,838.54)	(9,904.50)

	MAY	JUN	JUL	AUG
Bank Balance	(21,888.04)	(13,125.66)	5,028.82	49,703.40

	SEP	OCT	NOV	DEC
Bank Balance	67,813.43	63,592.47	60,721.51	53,250.55

Start up Capital required:

Owner's capital	£140,000
Mortgage	£50,000
Overdraft	£20,000

Sounds Right

Sounds Right are a small firm of amplifier manufacturers situated on the outskirts of Witney. The firm was set up two years ago and has already built up a good reputation for its range of amplifiers which are called Oxford, Truro and Edinburgh.

All the amplifiers are made using walnut vaneer but the firm has just received a letter from its suppliers stating that because of shipping problems they can only supply part of next month's consignment. The firm has calculated that next month they will only have sufficient veneer to make 124 cabinets.

Each amplifier also requires some skilled labour and some machine time. These are given below;

Model	Labour Hours	Machine Hours per speaker £	Contribution
Oxford	1	2	40
Truro	2	2	30
Edinburgh	4	1	25
Maximum hours available per month	330	200	

The contribution from the Oxford is high because the labour requirements are low but the firm does not expect to sell more that 40 Oxfords in any one month. There is a continuing large demand for the Truro and Edinburgh amplifiers.

You work for the firm in the Management Information Department and have been asked:

a   to formulate the linear programming model for Sounds Right production plan to maximise monthly contribution

b   set up the initial Simplex tableau and carry out the first iteration

c   give a full interpretation of the data below, given that it is the
final tableau for the above problem.

Final Tableau

XI	X2	X3	S1	S2	S3	S4	Quantity
0	0	1	2	0	-1	0	48
0	0	0	-6	1	+2	1	26
0	1	0	-1	0	-1	-1	36
1	0	0	0	0	0	1	40
0	0	0	20	0	5	10	3880

ZZX Limited and AOT Limited

The extract of the two firm's balance sheets are given below. Both companies operate in the same market and sell the same products. Last year they both made net profit after tax of £15,000. The only difference is their capital structure and this is shown below;

Extract of Balance Sheet for AOT Ltd as at 24 June 1988

Issued and Authorised Share Capital
170,000 £1.00 shares issued and
fully paid   170,000

Capital Employed   170,000

Extract of Balance Sheet of ZZX Ltd as at 24 June 1988

Issued and Authorised Share Capital
100,000 £1.00 shares issued and
fully paid   100,000

£40,000 10% Debenture Stock
repayable 2001 - 2007   40,000

£30,000 8% Unsecured Loan Stock
repayable 1998 - 2000   30,000

Capital Employed   170,000

You work as financial journalist for a local paper and have been asked by your editor to write an article about how the two companies are financed and the benefits and drawbacks of each method. Your article should be no more than 1,000 words and should be written for the layperson.

The Handy Chemist

The Handy Chemist is a small chain of ten chemist shops operating in the North West London suburbs. The firm stocks the usual range of cosmetics and other sundry items as well as a wide range of drugs which are prescribed by local general practitioners. To comply with legislation the chain have to keep some drugs which are rarely used but have high order costs. One such drug is codenamed QM28900X and the firm's records show that demand varies from five to nine prescriptions per week.

Demand Pattern for Drug QM28900X

Demand Prescriptions	5	6	7	8	9
Frequency	10	23	37	18	12

The wholesaler does not supply this drug on a regular basis but the order always arives at the end of the week ready for issue at the beginning of the following week. The lead time to receive an order is shown below:

Lead time in Weeks	2	3	4
Frequency	14	68	18

Each time an order is placed, the cost is £50.00 and the carrying cost is £0.20 per item per week, based on the lowest stock level of the week.

The firm's accountant has estimated that it costs the firm £4.00 per item every time the chain is out of stock at Head Office.

Handy Chemist's policy is to order 36 units of the drug at the end of the week during which the stock level falls to 18 units or less.

You work in the Management Information Department and have been asked by the accountant to calculate the firm's average stock level and the average weekly stockholding cost. You have decided to use the random numbers given below to simulate twelve weeks of trading and you know that the current stock holding of the drug at Head Office is 30 units.

Random Numbers

Demand	58	91	21	34	74	14	52	44	55	67	91	97

Lead Time	28	14	85

Highways Construction

Highways Construction have just won a contract for a traffic improvement scheme which involves widening a two mile stretch of road. The firm's surveyor has drawn up a list of the activities which must be completed and the firm's steam roller will be available to complete the activities A, B, and C.

You work for the firm as the Quantitative Analysis Manager and have been given the following memo from the Director of Engineering.

Memo

To   *Quantitative Analysis Manager*

From   *Director of Engineering*

As you know, we have just won the contract to widen Vine Road and have promised the council that the work will be completed in 115 days. Please bear in mind that time is of the essence, particularly with the holiday season fast approaching, so don't worry about having to hire any additional plant if that should prove necessary. However, as we have submitted tenders for other work I would like to complete this job ahead of schedule if possible and would be pleased if you could use the activity list to calculate the following;

1   draw the activity on node network for the project and determine the critical path

2   calculate the total free floats for each activity

3   each of the activities A, B and C require the use of a steamroller and unfortunately we only have one. This means that A, B and C can at best only be carried out in sequence, though in any order

4   how may days could be saved if we hired a steamroller?

Activity	Immediate Predeccessor	Duration in Days
A	-	13
B	-	23
C	-	15
D	A,B	9
E	-	18
F	C	17
G	F,E,H	46
H	D	24
I	F	42
J	D	59

Beese Engineering Limited

Beese Engineering Limited are a medium sized firm of marine engineers situated on the Gloucester to Sharpness canal. The firm specialise in repairs to pleasure boats and small coastal craft. They have just won a contract to remove the m.v. Frampton propeller and to carry out the main survey so that the ship can be classified to Bureau Veritas standards.

You work for the Management Information Department and have received the following memo from the Director of Engineering.

To   *Project Information Manager*

From   *Director Engineering*

As you know, the m.v. Frampton has arrived in dock for her main survey. The master is anxious to return to sea and we have agreed that the ship will be able to sail in thirty days' time. I have broken all of the work down into activities and they are as follows;

Activity	Immediately preceding activity(s)	Duration in days	Number of Engineers required
A	-	3	2
B	-	7	1
C	-	5	1
D	A	2	2
E	A	7	1
F	D	8	2
G	E,F	4	1
H	B,C,E,F	5	2
I	C	7	1
J	G,H,I	5	4
K	J	7	2
L	J	5	1

Can you please;

a   *draw an activity on node network for the project showing early and late activity times*

b   *determine the critical path and find the total float for each activity*

c   *draw a bar chart which shows each activity finishing as early as possible*

d   *write a report which I can give to the Chief Engineer stating how the activities can be completed in thirty days if only four engineers are available each day.*

Air Freight Packers Limited

Air Freight Packers was formed in 1980 by Derek Brown, Maria Gould and John Young. They had all worked for air freight companies in and around Heathrow and were convinced that there was a need for a small specialist packer of hazardous cargo.

At first, the three partners rented a small unit in Southall, close to the the airport, where the rent was reasonable. By August of that year, they had bought a van, leased a fork lift truck, and engaged four workers to start packing. Their first order was handling lighter fuel for the Gulf. Other work followed rapidly and gradually they built up a reputation for reliability and prompt delivery.

Derek knew that most packers received their orders from air freight agents around the airport. Before setting up the company, he approached several companies and told them about his plans. Reactions were very favourable but, nevertheless, all of the partners were a little apprehensive about leaving their old jobs and starting a new venture.

By Christmas 1981, Air Freight Packers was doing well. Orders were growing steadily and they were consistently beating their budget targets. Derek, Maria and John were confident that the new year would be successful.

1982 started well. New orders continued to pour in and Air Freight Packers began to win work from older and more established firms. In addition to the hazardous business, the firm was increasing its orders for general packing. By the end of the year this accounted from some forty per cent of turnover.

During the next five years the company engaged more staff to cope with expansion. Since 1987, the number of employees has remained constant and is shown in the organisation chart following.

Organisation Chart of Air Freight Packers (AFP)

By 1987, the company was large enough to support a management structure. The Directors split the firm into three areas: John Young is responsible for the day to day working of the unit, while Maria is in charge of marketing the company and for ensuring that customers' work is delivered and collected on time. Derek had been elected Managing Director because it was his idea to start the company and he is responsible for the firm's finances.

In July 1987, Maria visited 'Freight Pack' who were situated on the outskirts of Stanstead Airport. During her conversation with the owners she realised that they were finding it very hard to compete with more established packers in the area, and that they would like to be taken over by a larger firm of packers but keep management control of their Stanstead firm.

When Maria returned to AFP the three directors called an extraordinary general meeting at which it was decided to acquire Freight Pack and set up a new operation at Stanstead. The reasoning behind the decision was that Stanstead, as London's third airport, would experience a tremendous growth in traffic in the coming years. It was conveniently situated for the M25 and the Directors would find it relatively easy to visit their second area of operation. AFP made an offer of both shares and cash for Freight Pack, allowing its existing Directors to manage the company for a three year trial period.

This offer was put to the Directors of Freight Pack at the Caledonian Hotel in London in September and, after a short period of negotiation, the deal was accepted. The Directors believed that the acquisition would make their company one of the biggest packers of air freight in the coming years.

However, the expansion of the company caused problems. The unit in Southall was working to full capacity and often, during the summer months, work had to be carried on outside because the unit was too small to cope with the level of business.

In early 1988, the directors began to look for new premises near Heathrow Airport. One day they received details of a business park being built just south of Ashford. The new units were ideal, having good office space and ample car parking set in attractive parkland, allowing the firm to operate in pleasant surroundings.

The new premises are to be completed later in the year and will be sold on 100 year leases with rent reviews every five years. The Directors have calculated that they will need to raise an additional £120,000 and have approached their bank manager, Mr Patel. He has agreed to meet the Directors later this month with representatives from the bank's corporate finance division. The Directors are apprehensive about the meeting because they know that Mr Patel is cautious and expressed doubts about the firm growing too fast when it acquired Freight Pack.

The accounts of Air Freight Packers are given below together with additional financial information.

Task for Directors Air Freight Packing

You are to prepare such reports and accounting statements which you think are necessary for the meeting with Mr Patel and his representatives. At the meeting you will be required to present your information to the bank's delegation and answer any questions they may have.

Task for the bank's Corporate Finance Team

Your task is to scrutinise the accounts of Air Freight Packers and decide what additional information you require before the meeting. After you have listened to the Directors presentation, you must decide whether or not to lend the firm the money.

AIR FREIGHT PACKERS

Consolidated Balance Sheet at 31 March 1988

	1988 £	1987 £
Fixed Assets		
Tangible assets	79,641	69,654
Investments	9,333	7,524
	88,974	77,178
Current Assets		
Stocks	70,044	63,030
Debtors	64,206	56,847
Cash and Bank Balances	14,883	11,763
	149,133	131,640
Creditors		
Amounts falling due within one year	(70,590)	(71,028)
Net Current assets	78,543	60,612
Total assets less current liabilities	167,517	137,790
Creditors		
Amounts falling due after more than one year	(61,008)	(45,012)
Net assets	106,509	92,778
Capital and reserves		
Called up Share Capital	36,696	34,356
Share premium	19,134	12,978
Other reserves	40,911	37,665
Profit and loss	9,768	7,779
Sharehaolders' Funds	106,509	92,778

Notes to the Balance Sheet at 31 March 1988

	1988 £	1987 £
Creditors		
Amounts falling due within one year		
Trade Creditors	47,871	46,248
Corporation Tax	3,786	5.667
A.C.T.	5,928	4,725
Short Loans	9,000	10,977
Dividends	4,005	3,411
	70,590	71,028
Amounts falling due after more than one year		
Loan Capital	56,523	39,813
Corporation Tax	6,195	5,457
Deferred Tax	4,218	4,467
ACT recoverable	(5,928)	(4,725)
	61,008	45,012

The following additional information is available:

i) No interim dividends were paid by Air Freight Packers during this year.

ii) All taxation was paid as it became due, and in the year to 31 March 1987 Corporation Tax paid amounted to £5,466.

iii) Depreciation provided during the year amounted to £8,187 and fixed assets with a net book value of £2,544 were sold for £2,250.

iv) The acquisition of Freight Pack on 31 September 1987 was paid for by a share exchange and cash as follows:

Share issue, including premium	8,496
Cash	594
	9,090

v)   The Balance Sheet of Freight Pack at 31 March 1987 appeared as follows:

	£	£
Fixed Assets		4,677
Current Assets		
Stocks	5,364	
Debitors	3,561	
	8,925	
Creditors falling due		
within one year	4,512	4,413
Net Assets		9,090
Called up share capital	7,500	
Share Premium	750	
Profit and Loss	840	
Shareholders' funds		9,090

vi)   Included among "other reserves" is an Asset Replacement Reserve of £3,246 which had been created by a transfer from the Profit and Loss Account at 31 March 1987 in order to cover increased inflationary costs.

Hyde Engineering Limited

Hyde Engineering is a medium sized firm which manufactures metal bolts used in the car industry. The firm is based in Birmingham and last year celebrated its golden jubilee. During that period the Hyde's fortunes have tended to be tied to the car industry. In recent years they have tried to move away from the car industry by investing in plastic mouldings and selling these direct to wholesalers. This attempt has been successful with 20 per cent of the firm's sales now coming from this area of activity.

The Hyde firm has always enjoyed good labour relations. The last strike occurred twelve years ago and since then every new pay deal has been satisfactorily negotiated with the various unions. Each year the firm has to negotiate with the Amalgamated Union of Engineering Workers, the Transport and General Workers Union and the Association of Staff Technical and Managerial. The firm always negotiates in April with the A.U.E.W. and the level of pay award agreed on tends to set the trend for the other unions.

This year the Hyde's management knows that it will not be easy to arrive at a negotiated settlement. The level of pay rises in the industry has been running at 9 per cent while inflation, as recorded by the government's retail price index, has been at 6 per cent. Hyde Engineering has also had to compete strongly on price in order to keep existing contracts with major motor manufacturers in the area and knows that a high pay rise would mean that costs would have to rise. The firm is also suffering from import penetration in its plastic mouldings operation and wishes to invest £2,000,000 during the current fiscal year on new machinery to make them more productive.

The management and union representatives have agreed to meet in the conference rooms at the Barmouth Hotel on the outskirts of the city.

Management's Brief

The firm expects sales to rise by 10 per cent in the coming fiscal year and after tax profits to rise by 4 per cent. This means they can afford to pay an extra £500,000 in wages and benefits. The Management estimate that £120,000 will settle the wages bill when they negotiate with the other two unions.

They know that a large pay rise can only be financed by reducing the capital investment budget which in the long term will damage the firm's competiveness. The accountant has budgeted for a possible four week strike. It is, however, the Board's policy to try and avoid a strike because adverse publicity could result in lost orders with the motor manufacturers.

Pay Rise Costs

1   Each 1 per cent rise to the AUEW costs the firm £30,000

2   The firm employs 80 AUEW members

3   Subsidised canteen meals currently cost 50p and this costs the firm £80,000 a year.

4   Any price rise or fall in the canteen will have to be agreed with every union. As a result the management are reluctant to increase the subsidy.

5   Each extra day of holiday costs the firm £60,000 a year in wages and lost production.

6   A strike would cost the firm £50,000 a week in lost orders.

7   A reduction in hours worked would cost the firm £20,000 per hour per year.

8   The average weekly wage is £165 but the national average is £187.

Union Brief

The West Midlands have seen many small engineering firms either go bankrupt or merge with larger companies. As a result the union has seen a large reduction in its membership in the area.

A strike would cost £10,000 per week in strike benefit. In the present industrial climate it is thought that the workers are reluctant to strike. The background to union demands is:

1   Average earnings at Hyde Engineering are £165 a week as against a national average of £187. Pay rises in basic rates in the industry have averaged 9%.

2   The union estimate that each 1% rise in pay costs the firm £33,000.

3   Canteen meals to be pegged at 50p.

4   Some firms are paying Christmas bonuses to their staff and the union would like to negotiate a Christmas bonus. The average bonus in the industry has been £100 per worker.

5   The union would like to negotiate an extra day's holiday and reduce the working week by two hours.

The Thistle Wool Company Limited

The Thistle Wool Company was started by Mr Berry and his wife in 1879. At first they produced knitted woollen cardigans in the village of Cawdor just outside Inverness. Their products were well made, and soon the company established itself as a producer of quality woollens.

In 1890 Thistle bought a factory in Inverness and started to produce woollen blankets, kilts, women's skirts, pullovers and cardigans. The firm at this time employed twenty full-time employees and thirty part-time staff mainly knitting garments in their own homes.

Mr Berry died in 1907 at the age of sixty two, and the business was then run by his wife, son and daughter. The firm's sales and profits grew steadily, but tragedy hit the family business when the son, James Berry, was killed in the First World War in 1917 leaving Thistle in the hands of Mr Berry's wife Sara and her daughter Elizabeth who effectively ran the company. She was hardworking and efficient and had qualified as an accountant when she was twenty five. Elizabeth was determined to make Thistle a success and worked for the company until her death in 1978. In 1927, she married Andrew Giles and had two children, Joan and Sheila. Sheila inherited her mother's drive and business acumen, while Joan made a career as a successful novelist and took no part in the management of the company.

Under Elizabeth's management the company expanded. In the 1930's she bought a small Scottish distillery and sold whisky under the 'Highlander' brand name. During the Depression it was the distillery which subsidised the losses of the woollen mill. The Second World War changed the financial fortunes for the mill. Thistle won contracts from the Ministry of Defence for the supply of military clothing for the Scottish Regiments and was able to keep these contracts until defence cuts in the 1970s. In 1962,

Elizabeth acquired a small firm of cake and biscuit manufacturers which was renamed Elizabeth Berry Cake and Biscuit Limited.

Apart from expanding the business, Elizabeth completely reorganised the company and introduced a new management structure without surrendering family financial control. She left her share in the company to her children and made Sheila Managing Director before she died. The company has continued to trade successfully, and last year's pre-tax profits were 4.7 million on sales of 14 million.

The company is still organised as Elizabeth had decreed. Each subsidiary has a Manager who is also a Director of the main Board.

BOARD OF DIRECTORS

Sheila Giles

Managing Director. She has twenty years' experience with the company. Very dynamic, works hard, and is liked by the work force. Age 55.

James Faed

Director of Finance. Worked for the company since 1986. Helped finance the expansion of the company. Has good knowledge of external sources of finance, having previously worked for a large Scottish bank. Age 39.

John Weeks

Director of Manufacturing. He has worked for thirty seven years. Known to disagree with some of Sheila's expansion plans, but is a good worker and consistently meets production targets.

Carolyn Johnson

Company Secretary. Responsible for all administration. She has only been with the firm two years. Previously employed in a micro-computer company as an assistant company secretary. She is young for the post (age 25) but has proved to be a good appointment.

Robert Bryant

Sales Director. Only been with the company for four years. Has previously worked several fmcg* companies before joining Thistle Wool Company in 1981. He intends to retire in two years time.

Dennis Steadman

Director responsible for the "Highlander" Distillery. He has worked for the company for twelve years and was appointed Director in 1983. Age 42. He is very popular with his staff and has increased turnover at the distillery by 35% since his appointment.

Sue Tui San

Director responsible for Berry Cakes and Biscuits. She was appointed in 1982 and had previously worked for a food processing firm as Head of the Puddings Division. She is the only non-Scottish Director. Age 27.

* fmcg = fast moving consumer goods

Sales for the last five years

	1984 £m	1985 £m	1986 £m	1987 £m	1988 £m
Woollen Mill	1.5	1.8	2.3	2.9	4.5
Highlander Distillery	4.0	3.7	5.0	6.2	7.4
Elizabeth Berry Cakes	0.2	0.4	0.9	1.4	2.1

Group Employees - Full-Time

	1984	1985	1986	1987	1988
Woollen Mill	45	48	53	53	57
Highlander Distillery	30	30	35	35	42
Elizabeth Berry Cakes	20	27	32	40	40
	95	105	120	128	139

1988 was a record year with every Division turning in good results. The Distillery had its best year ever and was often referred to by the Board of Directors as the 'money machine'.

The firm has large cash balances earning interest on the London Money Market. Sheila however, does not like this and believes that past profits should be re-invested for the future.

At the last Board Meeting the Directors decided upon a plan of achieving future growth by acquisition. They particularly wished to expand the clothing division by diversifying into the lucrative sports and leisure wear market. As part of this policy the Board have been negotiating with the Directors of Fletcher's Tartan Ltd with the aim of purchasing their business.

Fletcher's Tartan is a relatively new company having been set up in the 1970s with a grant from the Scottish Development Agency. The firm produce a range of sports wear which is marketed under the "Leader" brand name and carrying the distinctive Fletcher's Tartan logo.

Note 1

FLETCHER'S TARTAN

Fletcher's Tartan was formed in 1972 by Stuart Henderson, Joan Westcoll and Mark Fletcher to manufacture high quality sportswear. (The three directors had all studied fashion and design and believed that there was a growing market for quality sportswear.)

The firm employs seventy people at its factory, situated on the outskirts of Dundee. Exports account for about 30% of the firm's sales but fluctuations in the exchange rate have lead to erratic earnings. Its two main export markets are the USA and West Germany.

The three Directors have been approached by Thistle, who would like to buy them out. Although they are keen to merge with a larger company, they want to retain management control and are asking for seats on the main Thistle Board. A meeting has been arranged at Thistle headquarters in Cawdor to discuss terms for the proposed acquisition.

Fletcher's Tartan Ltd

Balance Sheet as at 5th April 1988

Fixed Assets	Cost £000	Dep to date £000	Net Book Value £000
Freehold property	200		200
Plant & Machinery	75	15	60
Motor Vehicles	30	5	25
	305	20	285

Investments			
Treasury 14.5 1994			35
Treasury 11.5 2001-04			20
Current Assets			
Stock		60	
Debtors		30	
Bank & Cash Balances		15	
		105	
Less Current Liabilities			
Creditors		27	
Net Assets Employed			78
			418

Financed by:

200,000 Ord. £1 shares, authorised, called and fully paid.	200
75,000 9% Preference Shares of £1 each fully paid	75
General Reserve	65
Bank Term Loan 12%	78
	418

Notes to the Accounts

1 Fletcher's Tartan Ltd. profit after tax, before preference dividend, for the last five years have been:

	£000
1984	47
1985	32
1986	55
1987	62
1988	49

These figures include income from investments.

2 The firm's freehold property has been revalued and its new valuation is £240,000.

3 It is assumed that the value of the firm's assets other than Land & Buildings is its Net Book Value as shown in the balance sheets.

Thistle Wool Company
Consolidated Balance Sheet 5th April 1988

Fixed Assets	Cost	Dep to Date	Net Book Value
	£000	£000	£000
Freehold property	750	-	750
Machinery	350	75	275
Motor Vehicles	60	15	45
	1160	90	1070
Current Assets			
Stock		450	
Debtors		220	
Bank & Cash		175	
Investment		100	
		945	
Current liabilities			
Creditors	117		
Loan interest	7		
Dividends	20	144	801
Net Assets Employed			1871
Debentures 10% 2012-2014			506
			1365

Financed by:	
800,000 Ord.shares of £1 each fully paid Authorised and Issued	800
Share Premium	50
General Reserve	250
Consolidated Profit & Loss	120
	1220
Minority interest	45
Bank Term Loan	100
	1365

63

Note 2

Thistle Wool's Management Brief

You have invited the Directors of Fletcher's Tartan to meet you at your headquarters to negotiate the purchase price for Fletcher's Tartan and arranged a press conference afterwards to announce the outcome.

At the meeting you will have to negotiate for the best possible terms. You need to show:

a)   the price which the company should pay to purchase 100% of the ordinary shares,

b)   how the firm proposes to finance the payment for Fletcher's Tartan shares.

Note 3

Fletcher's Tartan Management Brief

You have agreed to meet the directors of Thistle Wool at their headquarters in Cawdor and to hold a press conference after the meeting to discuss the outcome of the negotations.

At the meeting you will have to negotiate for the best possible terms. You need to show:

a) what price the Thistle Wool Company should pay for Fletcher's Tartan,

b) the benefits which such a merger would bring about,

c) reasons why you should be allowed to manage the company and be given a seat on the main Board.

Sarah Jane Limited

Sarah Jane Limited is a successful manufacturer of ladies' clothes. The firm was founded in 1964 by two women, Sarah Towers and Jane Wilson who realised that there was a growing demand for quality clothing. They had both studied fashion and, when they finished their course, returned to their home town of Leicester where they started to make women's blouses in a rented garage. The two women used to sell the blouses in the local market and found that they were in high demand because of their design and price.

From 1966 to 1986 the firm rented a series of units. Sarah Jane grew and extended its product range to include not only women's blouses but also suits, skirts, overcoats, cardigans and jumpers. The products were sold under the SJ label in the United Kingdom, mainly to boutique and designer stores. In 1980, the firm began exporting its products to West Germany and France and has seen sales grow steadily.

In 1986 Sarah Jane decided to move to new premises and to purchase a new factory and cease renting units. The firm now employs over 200 people and is seen by the local council as one of the area's success stories.

In May of this year, the firm was approached by a well know United Kingdom High Street Store and asked if they would be prepared to manufacture men's suits. This would be a considerable departure from Sarah Jane's usual business, but the High Street Store believed that they were one of the few United Kingdom manufacturers to have the skill and specialised machinery which is essential for today's fashion conscious male market.

Sarah and Jane have decided to call in a firm of management consultants to help them decide whether to take this new order or continue with their existing products. You work as an assistant to the firm of consultants and have been supplied with the firm's last two sets of accounts, the terms of the High Street order and the expected returns from the new range of blouses. Your task is to answer Sarah Towers' and Jane Wilson's questions so that they can discuss the matter further at their next Board Meeting in July.

Terms of the Order

The High Street Store agrees to purchase the following men's suits over the next four years at the prices given below.

Year	Number of Suits	Price per Suit
1988	120,000	£50
1989	170,000	£49
1990	230,000	£43
1991	350,000	£38

Estimated Costs (£) of Manufacturing May 1988

	Mean Cost	Standard Deviation	Median Cost	Quartile Deviation
Cloth for each suit	14	2.90	13.50	2.12
Butons and twine	2	0.12	1.95	0.09
Direct Labour	4	1.20	4.10	0.95
Variable Overheads	7	1.12	6.95	1.01

Fixed Costs are estimated to be £120,000 per annum.

In Year 1 the suits are to be made in batches of 12,000. Materials to be paid for in month of production and payment will be made by the High Street Store one month after delivery. The first delivery is to be made in August 1988.

Internal Memo

From: *Amanda Shen*

Next week I am going to Scotland to help a firm with its job evaluation scheme. I will be returning next Wednesday and have agreed with the Directors of Sarah Jane that we will meet them on Monday. I will need your draft report to answer their questions for Thursday morning so that I can work on it over the weekend.

Thanks.

Amanda.

QUESTION 1

You are provided with the average manufacturing costs for May 1988. Compare and contrast the mean and median as measures of average and the standard deviation and quartile deviation semi interquartile range as measures of dispersion. Prepare a report which discusses the usefulness of the mean, median and mode to the clothing manufacture industry.

QUESTION 2

Prepare a report stating whether or not the firm should accept the order. Calculate the break even point for each of the four years.

QUESTION 3

Taking the data concerning the number of suits to be purchased by the High Street Store between 1988 and 1991 use a suitable statistical technique to determine how highly correlated the number of suits purchased is with time. If a high degree of corelation exists, determine the linear relationship between time and number of suits to be purchased and use the equation to predict how many suits will be purchased in 1992.

QUESTION 4

Assuming that the firm decides to go ahead with the order, they will need to borrow additional finance. I understand that the Directors are willing to increase their share capital by £40,000 and intend to borrow the balance from the bank. Draft a letter which can be sent to the bank requesting the loan and the purpose for which it is needed.

QUESTION 5

Given your prediction for the number of suits purchased in 1992, determine the likely cost that will be associated with the manufacture of those suits, assuming manufacturing costs do not rise.

Blenheim Road Garages Limited

Blenheim Road Garages Limited was founded by John Dixon in 1946 when he left the army after the Second World War. He had learnt to drive and how to repair engines whilst in the army and believed that there would be a good living in owning a small garage. John had persuaded his brother to join him and the two brothers ran the business until their retirement in 1985.

The garage was situated at a busy crossroads, and there were a number of small shops close by which meant that there was quite a lot of passing traffic. From the beginning, the garage sold petrol, repaired cars, did body work and sold second hand cars. John Dixon had always believed that the firm's strength lay in diversification but the post-war years had seen large changes in the garage trade. "Gas Bars" had almost displaced the old garage selling petrol and garage chains like "Kwik Fit" had taken away a sizeable proportion of the traditional garage business - customers liked to be able to watch their car being repaired and had become distrustful of garages. Fortunately, Blenheim Road Garages had not sold new cars because the heavy discounting had bankrupted many firms and profit margins were larger in second-hand vehicles.

Since 1985, the firm has been run by John Dixon's two children, Margaret and Paul. Paul studied mechanical engineering and Margaret completed a Business Studies Diploma at a London Polytechnic. Paul was in charge of the mechanical side of the firm and Margaret of the accounting side. Blenheim Road Garages also employed the following staff:

Present Organisation Chart of Blenheim Road Garages

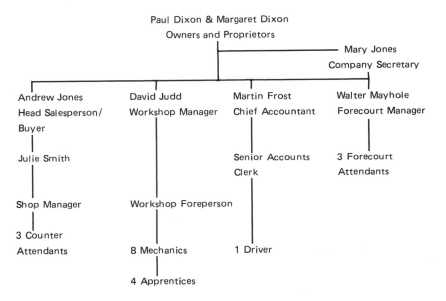

A major part of Blenheim Road Garage's present business involves servicing cars. Three types of services are offered:

1. Interim   Such a service is recommended every 5,000 miles or six months, whichever is sooner, and includes an oil change and change of oil filter plus checking for any other problems.   The charge of £35 includes the cost of oil and filter.

2. Regular   Recommended every 10,000 miles or annually. Includes the work carried out for an interim service plus changing spark plugs and points.   Material costs are included in the £50 charge.

3. Major   Recommended every 20,000 miles or every 2 years. In addition to the work carried out for the regular service brake fluid and coolant is changed.   A charge of £70 is made, to include material costs.

Resources used for the services are as follows:

	Interim	Regular	Major
Materials £			
Can of Oil	4.50	4.50	4.50
Oil Filter	1.50	1.50	1.50
Spark Plugs	-	4.00	4.00
Points	-	1.00	1.00
Brake Fluid	-	-	4.00
Coolant	-	-	4.00
Time (Hours)			
Mechanics	1.50	2.00	3.00
Apprentice	2.00	2.50	4.50
Maximum Demand (week)	120	60	40

Mechanics and appretices work a 40 hour week. As not all customers pay cash, Blenheim Road Garages does not allow more than £1,500 per week to pay for raw materials.

It had taken the company nearly forty years to grow to its present size. John Dixon hoped that his children would enjoy the same steady although unspectacular growth, but the early 1980s have been financially bad for the company and at times cash flow has been severe. Paul and Mary believe that the business cannot continue as it is into the 1990s and have an ambitious plan for the future.

In November of last year, a small factory at the back of the garage was put up for sale by the owners. Paul and Margaret Dixon are considering purchasing it and using the site to build an exhaust fitting and MOT Testing Centre.

The cost of purchasing the lease and redeveloping the site would be £50,000 and this sum would be payable in July. Dixons believe that, because of competition in the area, the first three months would be critical. They estimate the first three months expenses to be as follows:

1. Purchase of three new ramps in August for £6,000.

2. Purchase for Resale

   June £8,000   July £7,000   August £7,500
   These suppliers allow one month's credit.

3. Sales

   June £22,000   July £26,000   August £32,000

   The firm expects to sell 80% for cash, the balance being received within one month after sale.

4. Expenses and labour costs.
   These will be paid as they occur.

   June £9,000   July £10,000   August £7,200

5. Delivery Van
   This will cost £6,000 in July. You estimate its useful life to be four years.

6. Interest Payments - The firm has decided to save a certain amount each month to meet bank interest charges. The amounts are as follows:

   June £1,000   July £700   August £1,200

Car Sales obtain their present exhausts from three suppliers as follows:

Company	Cost per Unit (£)	Percentage Supplied
Wonder Exhausts	100	20
Super Exhausts	103	30
Bellco Exhausts	105	50

Experience suggests that the rate of return, due to faulty manufacture of exhausts by suppliers, is 1 in 40 for Wonder Exhausts, 1 in 50 for Super Exhausts and 1 in 80 for Bellco Exhausts.

The Dixons are also considering setting up a car wash. This would cost the firm £20,000 and have a life of ten years. It is estimated that an average of 212 cars per week would use the service. This figure, however is subject to a high level of variability with a standard deviation of 89. The estimated average costs and revenue are given below:

Water (heated)	40p per car
Soap	10p per car
Hot air drying	20p per car
Wax	5p per car
Fixed Costs of Car Wash	£5,000 per year
The cost of the Car Wash would be	£1.50

The family has decided to put another £30,000 into the business and proposes to borrow the balance from the bank. The Dixons however, are worried about the firm's financial position and the viability of the new ventures and have asked a local firm of management counsultants called JBS to look at their business. A copy of the firm's last two balance sheets are attached. You work as a trainee consultant at JBS have been asked to investigate various aspects of the firm's operations.

74

Blenheim Road Garages Limited

Balance Sheet as at 5 April 1988

Fixed Assets	1987	1988
Garage	70,000	70,000
Tools and Machinery	17,000	25,000
Motor Vehicles	10,000	17,000
Investments	15,000	15,000
Current Assets		
Stock	85,000	120,000
Debtors	23,000	32,000
Bank	32,000	
Cash	300	300
	252,300	279,300
Current Liabilities		
Creditors	82,300	84,000
Bank Overdraft		40,300
Net Assets		
Capital		
Share Capital		
(includes reserves)	110,000	115,000
Debentures 10%	40,000	40,000
Bank Term Loan	20,000	
	252,300	279,300

Extract from Car Sales Profit and Loss

	1987	1988
Sales	725,000	1,075,000
Trading Profit	110,000	156,300

Additional Notes

1. There have been no issues of shares during the year.

2. Dividend and taxation paid amounted to £41,300.

Internal Memo JBS Ltd

From: *Lara Judd, Director JBS*

Sorry to leave you this but I have got to go into hospital for an appendix operation this week. In ten days' time, I am meeting Margaret and Paul Dixon and will need a draft report on the following questions.

Thanks, Lara

QUESTION 1

Formulate Blenheim Road Garage's car servicing business as a linear programming problem to maximise the profit from this area.

A colleague has previously ran this problem using linear programming software and obtained the following results:

Final Tableau

X1	X2	X3	S1	S2	S3	S4	S5	S6	Qty
0	0	-.375	1	-.75	0	-.125	0	0	192.5
1	0	2.25	0	.5	0	-1.25	0	0	5
0	0	-2.25	0	-.5	1	1.25	0	0	115
0	1	0	0	0	0	1	0	0	60
0	0	1	0	0	0	0	1	0	40
0	0	5.5	0	-3	0	-3.5	0	1	810
0	0	6.25	0	14.5	0	2.75	0	0	2485

Where   X1 = number of interim services
        X2 = number of regular services
        X3 = number of major services
        S1 = slack in mechanics time
        S2 = slack in apprentices time
        S3 = slack in demand for interim services
        S4 = slack in demand for regular services
        S5 = slack in demand for major services
        S6 = slack in cash to purchase materials

Interpret the results, including the shadow prices, from the final tableau and hence advise Paul and Margaret how to optimise profits and improve profitability in the future.

QUESTION 2

Write a report to the Directors outlining how a system of budgetary control could help the company conserve its working capital. Your answer should include a cash budget showing the amount of additional capital which the firm will need to fund the new venture.

QUESTION 3

The average number of cars that it is estimated are likely to use the proposed car wash is subject to a high level of variablility. The Dixons wish to know what sorts of numbers to expect in practice and have asked you to calculate:

(i) the range within which the middle 50% of observations can be expected to fall.

(ii) the range within which the middle 95% of observations can be expected to fall.

QUESTION 4

Write a report to the Directors assessing the company's present use of capital. Your answer should include a Source and Application of Funds Statement.

QUESTION 5

Given the rate of return of the exhausts manufactured by Wonder, Super and Bellco Exhausts, Paul and Margaret wish to know the overall percentage of exhausts that are likely to be returned. They would also like you to calculate the probabilities that an exhaust returned as faulty originated from each of the respective manufacturers. Use the data in the Case Study to calculate the information required.

QUESTION 6

Write a report to the Directors outlining the importance of break even charts to management in decision making. Your answer should include a break even chart for the proposed car wash.

Summary of the Accounting Ratios in Common Use

1. Liquidity Ratios

The Current Ratio $\qquad = \qquad \dfrac{\text{Current Assets}}{\text{Current Liabilities}}$

Acid Test Ratio $\qquad = \qquad \dfrac{\text{Current Assets Less Stock}}{\text{Current Liabilities}}$

2. Profitability Ratios

Gross Profit to Sales $\qquad = \qquad \dfrac{\text{Gross Profit x 100}}{\text{Sales}}$

Gross Profit Margin to Sales (percentage)

$$= \dfrac{\text{Gross Profit for the year x 100}}{\text{Sales Turnover for the year}}$$

Net Profit to Sales $\qquad = \qquad \dfrac{\text{Net Profit x 100}}{\text{Sales}}$

Profit to Shareholders Investment

$$= \dfrac{\text{Profit after Taxation}}{\text{Shareholders Investment}}$$

Profit to Shareholders Investment, if the firm has Preference Shareholders

$$= \dfrac{\text{Profit after Taxation \& Preference Dividend}}{\text{Ordinary Issued Share Capital}}$$

Return on Capital Employed (percentage)

$$= \dfrac{\text{Profit (before interest on debts) x 100}}{\text{Net Capital Employed}}$$

Interest Turnover Ratio $\qquad = \qquad \dfrac{\text{Total Profit (before Tax)}}{\text{Interest Paid}}$

$$\text{Profit per Employee} = \frac{\text{Operating Profit for the year}}{\text{Average no. of Employees}}$$

3. Use of Assets

$$\text{Fixed Assets Turnover Ratio} = \frac{\text{Sales turnover for the year}}{\text{Average Net Book Value of Fixed Assets}}$$

$$\text{Net Assets to Fixed Assets} = \frac{\text{Net Current Assets}}{\text{Fixed Assets}}$$

$$\text{Stock Turnover Ratio} = \frac{\text{Cost of Goods Sold}}{\text{Stock}}$$

$$\text{Sales per Employee} = \frac{\text{Sales Turnover for the period}}{\text{Average no. of Employees}}$$

$$\text{Sales to Debtors} = \frac{\text{Sales}}{\text{Debtors}}$$

$$\text{Bad Debts Ratio} = \frac{\text{Bad Debts incurred} \times 100}{\text{Sales Turnover on Credit}}$$

4. Capital Ratios

$$\text{Gearing Ratio} = \frac{\text{Debt Capital}}{\text{Equity Capital}}$$

$$\text{Fixed Capital Ratio} = \frac{\text{Average Long-term Capital for the year}}{\text{Average Fixed Assets for the year}}$$

$$\text{Shareholders investment} = \frac{\text{Shareholders Investment}}{\text{Total Assets}}$$

5. Investment Ratios

$$\text{Earnings per Share} = \frac{\text{Profit after Tax \& Preference Share Dividend}}{\text{No. of Issued Ordinary Shares}}$$

Dividend Yield $=$ $\dfrac{\text{Ordinary Share Dividend per Share} \times 100}{\text{Market Price per Share}}$

Dividend Cover $=$ $\dfrac{\text{Profit after Tax less Preference Share Dividend}}{\text{Gross Dividend on Ordinary Shares}}$

Price Earnings $=$ $\dfrac{\text{Present Market Price per Ordinary Share}}{\text{Annual Earnings per Share}}$

Prescribed formats for company accounts

Balance sheet - format 1

A. **Called up share capital not paid**

B. **Fixed assets**

I **Intangible assets**
 1. Development costs
 2. Concessions, patents, licences, trade marks and similar rights and assets.
 3. Goodwill
 4. Payments on account

II **Tangible assets**
 1. Land and buildings
 2. Plant and machinery
 3. Fixtures, fittings, tools and equipment
 4. Payments on account and assets in course of construction

III **Investments**
 1. Shares in group companies
 2. Loans to group companies
 3. Shares in related companies
 4. Loans to related companies
 5. Other investments other than loans
 6. Other loans
 7. Own shares

C. **Current assets**

I **Stocks**
 1. Raw materials and consumables
 2. Work in progress
 3. Finished goods and goods for resale
 4. Payments on account

II **Debtors**
 1. Trade debtors
 2. Amounts owed by group companies
 3. Amounts owed by related companies
 4. Other debtors
 5. Called up share capital not paid
 6. Prepayments and accrued income

III **Investments**
 1. Shares in group companies
 2. Own shares

3. Other investments
IV   **Cash at bank and in hand**
D.   **Prepayments and Accrued income**
E.   **Creditors: amounts falling due within one year**
    1. Debenture loans
    2. Bank loans and overdrafts
    3. Payments received on account
    4. Trade creditors
    5. Bills of exchange payable
    6. Amounts owed to group companies
    7. Amounts owed to related companies
    8. Other creditors including taxation and social security
    9. Accruals and deferred income
F.   **Net current assets (liabilities)**
G.   **Total assets less current liabilities**
H.   **Creditors: amounts falling due after more than one year**
    1. Debenture loans
    2. Bank loans and overdrafts
    3. Payments received on account
    4. Trade creditors
    5. Bills of exchange payable
    6. Amounts owed to group companies
    7. Amounts owed to related companies
    8. Other creditors including taxation and social security
    9. Accruals and deferred income
I.   **Provisions for liabililties and charges**
    1. Pensions and similar obligations
    2. Taxation, including deferred taxation
    3. Other provisions
J.   **Accruals and deferred income**
K.   **Capital and reserves**
I   **Called up share capital**
II   **Share premium account**
III   **Revaluation reserve**
IV   **Other reserves**
    1. Capital redemption reserve
    2. Reserve for own shares
    3. Reserves provided for by the articles of association
    4. Other reserves
V   **Profit and loss account**

83

Profit and loss account - formats 1 and 2

Format 1
1. Turnover
2. Cost of Sales
3. Gross profit or loss
4. Distribution costs
5. Administrative expenses
6. Other operating income
7. Income from shares in group companies
8. Income from shares in related companies
9. Income from other fixed asset investments
10. Other interest receivable and similar income
11. Amounts written off investments
12. Interest payable and similar charges
13. Tax on profit or loss on ordinary activities
14. Profit or loss on ordinary activities after taxation
15. Extraordinary income
16. Extraordinary charges
17. Extraordinary profit or loss
18. Tax on extraordinary profit or loss
19. Other taxes not shown under the above items
20. Profit or loss for the financial year

Format 2

1. Turnover
2. Change in stocks of finished goods and in work in progress
3. Own work capitalised
4. Other operating income
5. (a) Raw materials and consumables
   (b) Other external charges
6. Staff costs:
   (a) wages and salaries
   (b) social security costs
   (c) other pension costs
7. (a) Depreciation and other amounts written off tangible and intangible fixed assets
   (b) Exceptional amounts written off current assets
8. Other operating charges

9. Income from shares in group companies
10. Income from shares in related companies
11. Income from other fixed asset investments
12. Other interest receivable and similar income
13. Amounts written off investments
14. Interest payable and similar charges
15. Tax on profit or loss on ordinary activities
16. Profit or loss on ordinary activities after taxation
17. Extraordinary income
18. Extraordinary charges
19. Extraordinary profit or loss
20. Tax on extraordinary profit or loss
21. Other taxes not shown under the above items
22. Profit or loss for the financial year

Glossary

Accounting

The system of recording financial information usually using the system of double entry book-keeping thereby allowing interested parties to make financial decisions.

Accounting Equation

The assets of a firm are equal to its liabilities. Assets are things which the firm owns even if it has not yet paid for them and liabilities are claims against the firm.

Accounts Receivable

A firm's credit sales to customers.

Acid Test Ratio

Current assets less stock/Current Liabilities. This ratio shows the firm's ability to meet its short term liabilities.

Annual Accounts

The set of accounts comprising the balance sheet together with a profit and loss and statement of source and application of funds.

Assets

Everything of value owned by a business.

Authorised Share

This is the amount of money which the company took power to raise when it was formed. Most companies do not raise the full amount of their authorised share capital when they are incorporated.

Balance Sheet

A statement showing a firm's assets and liabilities as at a certain date.

Bear

A person who believes that share prices will fall.

Bond

A certificate showing the indebtedness of an organisation together with the rate of interest payable and the date the loan will be repaid.

Bonus Issue

The issuing of shares to existing shareholders by distributing a company's reserves as shares.

86

Book Value	The historical cost of an asset less depreciation accumulated over the asset's life.
Break Even	The amount of sales needed to cover a firm's fixed and variable costs. Above the break even point the firm makes its profit and below it makes a loss.
Bull	A person who believes that share prices will rise.
Called Up Capital	This refers to shares issued by the company but not yet fully paid for by the shareholders.
Capital	The money which is financing the business.
Capital Employed	The long term capital which finances a firm. It includes share capital, reserves and loan capital.
Capital Expenditure	Money spent by the company on purchasing fixed assets.
Capital Loss	Losses made on the sale of fixed assets.
Capital Profit	Profit made on the sale of fixed assets.
Capital Receipts	Money received by a company on the issue of shares and debentures.
Cash Flow	Accounting term used to describe the cash generated and used during a given financial period.
Contingent Liability	Obligation which may arise in respect of past or future events (the outcome of a law case).
Corporation Tax	Tax calculated on a company's profits.
Cumulative Preference Shares	These shares allow the owners to receive arrears of dividend before dividends are paid to the ordinary shareholders.
Current Assets	These are assets of a circulating nature which are acquired by a business in order to trade with other companies or individuals.

87

Examples are stock, debtors (people who owe the company money) bank and cash balances.

Debenture

Normally a secured loan over the assets of a company. In recent years some well known companies have issued unsecured debentures. The debenture holders do not own the company but they are entitled to interest payments. If the interest due to them is not paid, they can take steps to liquidate the company.

Depreciation

Many assets can be assumed to fall in value over a period of years; machinery wears out, buildings deteriorate. An allowance called depreciation for this fall in value must be included in the final accounts.

Fixed Assets

Assets which are held by a company on a long basis (for more than one year) to enable the company to generate income and profit. These assets are not bought primarily for resale.

Floating Debenture

Secured loan over the floating assets of a company (usually stock).

Gearing

The ratio of a firm's debt to equity capital. In the USA it is called leverage.

Goodwill

Sum of money paid for the good name of a business. When a business is purchased any amount paid in excess of its net worth represents the value placed on goodwill.

Gross Profit

The profit made on goods and services sold before expenses are deducted.

Historical Cost

The original cost of acquiring the fixed asset.

Issued Share

This is the amount of money which the shareholders have actually put into the company.

Liquid Asset

Cash and any other asset which can be converted quickly into cash.

Listed Investment

An investment which is quoted on a recognised stock exchange, e.g. London, Tokyo, New York.

Minority Interest	Shares held in a subsidiary company by shareholders other than a holding company or its nominees.
Net Profit	The gross profit less expenses.
Nominal Value	The face value of a share or loan stock.
Ordinary Shareholders	These are the owners of the company. They are entitled to a dividend, which is a share of the firm's profit.
Paid Up Capital	This refers to shares which have been issued by the company and which have been fully paid for by the shareholders.
Preference Shareholders	Owners of these shares enjoy preferential rights over the ordinary shareholders. Their dividend is normally at a pre-deteremined rate and is payavble before payment to the ordinary shareholders. The Articles of Association sometimes make special provision for the preference shareholders by allowing them to be repaid in full before the ordinary shareholders in the event of the company being wound up. If there is no such provision then all shareholders share equally the remaining assets of the company.
Reserves	These are unappropriated profits or surplus funds made possible by the revaluation of fixed assets or the issue of shares for more than their nominal value.
Retained Profit	Profits retained in the business, and which are not being distributed to the shareholders as dividends.
Revenue Reserve	These consist of undistributed profits and can be used to pay dividends, maintain the business, absorb losses or they can be distributed to the shareholders as bonus shares. The revenue reserve is made up of the general reserve and the profit and loss account in the balance sheet.
Rights Issue	The raising of new capital by inviting existing shareholders to subscribe for new shares on preferential terms.
Share Premium	This shows that the shares were once sold for more than their

nominal value and the surplus is shown in the balance sheet as a capital reserve.

Shareholders' Funds   This is the total amount of money which belongs to the shareholders i.e. share capital plus reserves.

Sinking Fund   A fund created for the redemption of a liability. The aim is to set aside a certain sum which will at a certain date in the future pay off the debt.

Unappropriated Profits   Profits which the company has reinvested in the firm, instead of distributing them as dividends to the shareholders.

Unlisted Investment   An investment which is not quoted on a recognised stock exchange.

Unsecured Loan   Loan stock which carries interest but is not secured on any of the assets of the company.

Working Capital   The difference between a firm's current assets and its current liabilities.

DCF TABLES

Compound Sum of £1 (CVIF) $S = P(1 + r)^N$

Period	1%	2%	3%	4%	5%	6%	7%
1	1.010	1.020	1.030	1.040	1.050	1.060	1.070
2	1.020	1.040	1.061	1.082	1.102	1.124	1.145
3	1.030	1.061	1.093	1.125	1.158	1.191	1.225
4	1.041	1.082	1.126	1.170	1.216	1.262	1.311
5	1.051	1.104	1.159	1.217	1.276	1.338	1.403
6	1.062	1.126	1.194	1.265	1.340	1.419	1.501
7	1.072	1.149	1.230	1.316	1.407	1.504	1.606
8	1.083	1.172	1.267	1.369	1.477	1.594	1.718
9	1.094	1.195	1.305	1.423	1.551	1.689	1.838
10	1.105	1.219	1.344	1.480	1.629	1.791	1.967
11	1.116	1.243	1.384	1.539	1.710	1.898	2.105
12	1.127	1.268	1.426	1.601	1.796	2.012	2.252
13	1.138	1.294	1.469	1.665	1.886	2.133	2.410
14	1.149	1.319	1.513	1.732	1.980	2.261	2.579
15	1.161	1.346	1.558	1.801	2.079	2.397	2.759
16	1.173	1.373	1.605	1.873	2.183	2.540	2.952
17	1.184	1.400	1.653	1.948	2.292	2.693	3.159
18	1.196	1.428	1.702	2.026	2.407	2.854	3.380
19	1.208	1.457	1.754	2.107	2.527	3.026	3.617
20	1.220	1.486	1.806	2.191	2.653	3.207	3.870
25	1.282	1.641	2.094	2.666	3.386	4.292	5.427
30	1.348	1.811	2.427	3.243	4.322	5.743	7.612

Period	8%	9%	10%	12%	14%	15%	16%
1	1.080	1.090	1.100	1.120	1.140	1.150	1.160
2	1.166	1.186	1.210	1.254	1.300	1.322	1.346
3	1.260	1.295	1.331	1.405	1.482	1.521	1.561
4	1.360	1.412	1.464	1.574	1.689	1.749	1.811
5	1.469	1.539	1.611	1.762	1.925	2.011	2.100
6	1.587	1.677	1.772	1.974	2.195	2.313	2.436
7	1.714	1.828	1.949	2.211	2.502	2.660	2.826
8	1.851	1.993	2.144	2.476	2.853	3.059	3.278
9	1.999	2.172	2.358	2.773	3.252	3.518	3.803
10	2.159	2.367	2.594	3.106	3.707	4.046	4.411
11	2.332	2.580	2.853	3.479	4.226	4.652	5.117
12	2.518	2.813	3.138	3.896	4.818	5.350	5.926
13	2.720	3.066	3.452	4.363	5.492	6.153	6.886
14	2.937	3.342	3.797	4.887	6.261	7.076	7.988
15	3.172	3.642	4.177	5.474	7.138	8.137	9.266
16	3.426	3.970	4.595	6.130	8.137	9.358	10.748
17	3.700	4.328	5.054	6.866	9.276	10.761	12.468
18	3.996	4.717	5.560	7.690	10.575	12.375	14.463
19	4.316	5.142	6.116	8.613	12.056	14.232	16.777
20	4.661	5.604	6.728	9.646	13.743	16.367	19.461
25	6.848	8.623	10.835	17.000	26.462	32.919	40.874
30	10.063	13.268	17.449	29.960	50.950	66.212	85.850

Present Value of £1 (PVIF) $P = S(1 + r)^{-N}$

Period	1%	2%	3%	4%	5%	6%	7%	8%	9%	10%	12%	14%	15%
1	0.990	0.980	0.971	0.962	0.952	0.943	0.935	0.926	0.917	0.909	0.893	0.877	0.870
2	0.980	0.961	0.943	0.925	0.907	0.890	0.873	0.857	0.842	0.826	0.797	0.769	0.756
3	0.971	0.942	0.915	0.889	0.864	0.840	0.816	0.794	0.772	0.751	0.712	0.675	0.658
4	0.961	0.924	0.889	0.855	0.823	0.792	0.763	0.735	0.708	0.683	0.636	0.592	0.572
5	0.951	0.906	0.863	0.822	0.784	0.747	0.713	0.681	0.650	0.621	0.567	0.519	0.497
6	0.942	0.888	0.838	0.790	0.746	0.705	0.666	0.630	0.596	0.564	0.507	0.456	0.432
7	0.933	0.871	0.813	0.760	0.711	0.665	0.623	0.583	0.547	0.513	0.452	0.400	0.376
8	0.923	0.853	0.789	0.731	0.677	0.627	0.582	0.540	0.502	0.467	0.404	0.351	0.327
9	0.914	0.837	0.766	0.703	0.645	0.592	0.544	0.500	0.460	0.424	0.361	0.308	0.284
10	0.905	0.820	0.744	0.676	0.614	0.558	0.508	0.463	0.422	0.386	0.322	0.270	0.247
11	0.896	0.804	0.722	0.650	0.585	0.527	0.475	0.429	0.388	0.350	0.287	0.237	0.215
12	0.887	0.788	0.701	0.625	0.557	0.497	0.444	0.397	0.356	0.319	0.257	0.208	0.187
13	0.879	0.773	0.681	0.601	0.530	0.469	0.415	0.368	0.326	0.290	0.229	0.182	0.163
14	0.870	0.758	0.661	0.577	0.505	0.442	0.388	0.340	0.299	0.263	0.205	0.160	0.141
15	0.861	0.743	0.642	0.555	0.481	0.417	0.362	0.315	0.275	0.239	0.183	0.140	0.123
16	0.853	0.728	0.623	0.534	0.458	0.394	0.339	0.292	0.252	0.218	0.163	0.123	0.107
17	0.844	0.714	0.605	0.513	0.436	0.371	0.317	0.270	0.231	0.198	0.146	0.108	0.093
18	0.836	0.700	0.587	0.494	0.416	0.350	0.296	0.250	0.212	0.180	0.130	0.095	0.081
19	0.828	0.686	0.570	0.475	0.396	0.331	0.276	0.232	0.194	0.164	0.116	0.083	0.070
20	0.820	0.673	0.554	0.456	0.377	0.312	0.258	0.215	0.178	0.149	0.104	0.073	0.061
25	0.780	0.610	0.478	0.375	0.295	0.233	0.184	0.146	0.116	0.092	0.059	0.038	0.030
30	0.742	0.552	0.412	0.308	0.231	0.174	0.131	0.099	0.075	0.057	0.033	0.020	0.015

Present Value of £1 (PVIF) $P = S(1 + r)^{-N}$ cont.

Period	16%	18%	20%	24%	28%	32%	36%	40%	50%	60%	70%	80%	90%
1	0.862	0.847	0.833	0.806	0.781	0.758	0.735	0.714	0.667	0.625	0.588	0.556	0.526
2	0.743	0.718	0.694	0.650	0.610	0.574	0.541	0.510	0.444	0.391	0.346	0.309	0.277
3	0.641	0.609	0.579	0.524	0.477	0.435	0.398	0.364	0.296	0.244	0.204	0.171	0.146
4	0.552	0.516	0.482	0.423	0.373	0.329	0.292	0.260	0.198	0.153	0.120	0.095	0.077
5	0.476	0.437	0.402	0.341	0.291	0.250	0.215	0.186	0.132	0.095	0.070	0.053	0.040
6	0.410	0.370	0.335	0.275	0.227	0.189	0.158	0.133	0.088	0.060	0.041	0.029	0.021
7	0.354	0.314	0.279	0.222	0.178	0.143	0.116	0.095	0.059	0.037	0.024	0.016	0.011
8	0.305	0.266	0.233	0.179	0.139	0.108	0.085	0.068	0.039	0.023	0.014	0.009	0.006
9	0.263	0.226	0.194	0.144	0.108	0.082	0.063	0.048	0.026	0.015	0.008	0.005	0.003
10	0.227	0.191	0.162	0.116	0.085	0.062	0.046	0.035	0.017	0.009	0.005	0.003	0.002
11	0.195	0.162	0.135	0.094	0.066	0.047	0.034	0.025	0.012	0.006	0.003	0.002	0.001
12	0.168	0.137	0.112	0.076	0.052	0.036	0.025	0.018	0.008	0.004	0.002	0.001	0.001
13	0.145	0.116	0.093	0.061	0.040	0.027	0.018	0.013	0.005	0.002	0.001	0.001	0.000
14	0.125	0.099	0.078	0.049	0.032	0.021	0.014	0.009	0.003	0.001	0.001	0.000	0.000
15	0.108	0.084	0.065	0.040	0.025	0.016	0.010	0.006	0.002	0.001	0.000	0.000	0.000
16	0.093	0.071	0.054	0.032	0.019	0.012	0.007	0.005	0.002	0.001	0.000	0.000	
17	0.080	0.060	0.045	0.026	0.015	0.009	0.005	0.003	0.001	0.001	0.000		
18	0.069	0.051	0.038	0.021	0.012	0.007	0.004	0.002	0.001	0.000			
19	0.060	0.043	0.031	0.017	0.009	0.005	0.003	0.002	0.001	0.000			
20	0.051	0.037	0.026	0.014	0.007	0.004	0.002	0.001	0.000	0.000			
25	0.024	0.016	0.010	0.005	0.002	0.001	0.000	0.000					
30	0.012	0.007	0.004	0.002	0.001	0.000	0.000						

Notes

Notes

Notes

A Manager's Guide to Quantitative Methods

Michael Cuming

isbn 0 946139 01 6   £8.90   Paperback

An unusual and comprehensive introduction to
quantitative methods using topical examples
and diagrams to analyse real problems
and suggest solutions.

A user-friendly book for managers who need
to appreciate the uses, misuses and potentialities
of quantitative methods.

CONTENTS

Frequency distributions
Getting the right answer from your calculator
Summarising distributions
The language of uncertainty
Simplifying data
Compound interest and discounting
Correlation and regression
Tracking things in time
Finding out by sampling
Drawing conclusions
Managing with the computer
Problems with data

'Overall this book is a comprehensive guide to quantitative
methods and *truly should require no previous mathematical
knowledge...* It is worth serious consideration for
a wide range of management courses.
V.J. Seddon in *Natfhe Journal* February, 1985.

MRS THATCHER'S CASEBOOK

Non-partisan studies in Conservative Government policy

Terry Garrison

Well-researched case studies of ten major crises handled
by Mrs Thatcher's government.

Inner city time bomb ?
The Falklands War
GCHQ
Deregulation of the buses
London Transport - Fares Fair
The coal strike
Flexible rostering - British Rail
British Steel
The De Lorean dream
British Leyland

Includes a large section on policy analysis for managers.

Hardback binding   £19.95 (student edition/bulk £9.95)
isbn 0 946139 86 5

TUTOR'S PACK

Case notes, chronologies, commentary and other material
to supplement, support and extend the text.

Presentation looseleaf binder   £59.00 (gratis with 15 books)
isbn 0 946139 46 6